Richard Twining

Observations on the Tea and Window Act and on the Tea Trade

Richard Twining

Observations on the Tea and Window Act and on the Tea Trade

ISBN/EAN: 9783744728263

Printed in Europe, USA, Canada, Australia, Japan

Cover: Foto ©Suzi / pixelio.de

More available books at **www.hansebooks.com**

OBSERVATIONS

ON THE

Tea and Window Act,

AND ON

The TEA TRADE.

By RICHARD TWINING.

——" ita uti res eſt, dicere."
TERENCE.

———————

LONDON:

Printed for T. CADELL, in the Strand.

M DCC LXXXIV.

OBSERVATIONS

ON THE

Tea and Window Act,

&c. &c.

IT too frequently happens, that the Public find it difficult to obtain clear and satisfactory information, upon those subjects which materially concern them: and whilst Truth is with-held by some, and Falsehood industriously circulated by others, it is no wonder if the opinions which are adopted, and the decisions which are formed, should be erroneous. This Error ought to be corrected, rather than blamed; for what right have we to expect, that no attention should be paid to the information which *is* produced, because more authentic information *may* be produced? or that no judgement should be suffered to pass upon the evidence which *is* collected, because it is possible that more complete evidence *may* be collected hereafter? If, however, such Errors, when they arise in common life, are not to be blamed, or at least not

A   with

with a philofophical feverity, yet they ought, undoubtedly, to be corrected: and the proper mode of correcting them, is, by producing Truth, and oppofing it to Falfehood. But here difficulties are apt to arife; and that communication of circumftantial Truth, which is neceffary to the elucidation of any particular fubject, cannot, in many inftances, be looked for, except from thofe perfons who are fo intimately connected with that fubject, that their impartiality is immediately queftioned: and it may be, that Truth itfelf, coming from fuch a quarter, will meet with a much lefs favourable reception in the world, than anonymous Falfehood.

I am well aware that this reafoning is peculiarly applicable to myfelf, when I venture to deliver to the Public any information, or any opinion, relative to the fubject of Tea. It is, I confefs, a fubject which is placed fo near to me, that fome doubt may reafonably be entertained, whether I can view it in a juft light. I will only fay, that I have moft carefully endeavoured to do fo, by removing myfelf, as nearly as poffible, to the proper point of diftance; and as the thing, however difficult, is by no means impoffible, I requeft that the Public will not prejudge my failure in this attempt at Impartiality. I have watched myfelf narrowly: I expect to be, and I even wifh to be, watched narrowly by others; and fhould it be found, that whilft I am endeavouring to prevent the adoption of prejudices, I am under the influ-

ence

ence of them myfelf, I readily confefs that I fhall then merit the fevereft reproof.

There is one other fufpicion which I wifh to guard againft: it is that of my being biaffed by party opinions. The very idea of a perfon in my humble fituation of life, attaching himfelf to a Party, and fancying that he is capable of affording it fervice and fupport, is, I confefs, perfectly ridiculous. And yet fuch things, ridiculous as they may feem, are believed actually to happen: and I have already been told, more than once, that in the unimportant part which I have hitherto taken in this bufinefs, I have been guided, not by principle, but by party attachments, or even party influence. This is an opinion which I am anxious to remove, becaufe, whilft it is entertained, I cannot poffibly be thought deferving of a moment's attention. I fhould, it is true, receive fatisfaction, let who would be Minifter, in promoting any plan of general utility. And, unlefs the wheel of Government were very cracked and crazed indeed, I would rather be the unaf-fuming fly that goes *with* it, than the impertinent pebble that endeavours to obftruct its motion. It is true, that I have frequently waited upon Mr. Pitt, and that Mr. Pitt has afked me many queftions relative to the Tea-trade. I have anfwered them as fairly and as explicitly as I could: I truft, with-out rudenefs; I am fure, without fervility: and if any other Minifter had thought proper to confult me upon a fubject, which thus nearly concerned my own profeffion, and the Public in general, I would have given to him, as I have done to the

prefent

present Minister, the best information in my power. But it is high time to quit this Introduction, and to hasten to that subject to which it is intended to lead.

I believe it will be generally allowed, that the late Act of Parliament, by which an alteration was made in the duties upon Tea, and an additional duty was laid upon Windows, does, at this moment, very much engage the public attention. In order to throw, if possible, some light upon this subject, I would wish to consider, in the first place, what was the original Cause, and also the Intent of this Bill; to shew, in the second place, in what respects it has hitherto failed, and the causes of that failure; and lastly, to point out, as far as it may be in my power, those methods which are most likely to correct this failure; to remove the principal objections that are made to this Act, and to render it productive of the good purposes for which it was framed.

That the *cause* of this Bill may be properly understood, it will be necessary to recollect, that the East India Company possess an exclusive right of supplying Great Britain and Ireland, and the Dependencies of Great Britain, with Tea. Of this right the Company have been so far deprived, and the Smuggler has become so formidable a rival, that, upon the most moderate computation, they shared the Tea-trade equally between them; and, according to some calculations, the Smuggler had two thirds of it. This infringement upon the commerce of the East India Company was, clearly, a matter

matter of very great importance to themfelves; it was alfo an evil which fo materially affected Government, and the Public in general, that fome remedy appeared to be indifpenfably neceffary. The article of Tea had been fo repeatedly an object of taxation, that the duty upon it amounted, at length, to very nearly cent. per cent. : and fuch a temptation was confequently held out for the evafion of this duty, that the utmoft rigor of the Excife Laws afforded but a very feeble check to it. Nay more, thofe Excife Laws, which had been framed for the fuppreffion of this evil, were converted, by the wifdom of the difobedient, into its protection : and the fame Permit which was granted for the Teas of the Eaft India Company, fheltered thofe of the Smuggler. To fo great a height had this illegal traffic been carried, that dealers, refiding even in the Capital, could almoft conftantly purchafe very large quantities of Tea, which, it was well known, had never paid any duty; and which neverthelefs came into the dealer's fhop, with as regular a Permit, and with as much fafety, as if the goods had been delivered from the warehoufes of the Eaft India Company, and had paid the full duties. Nor was this trade confined to perfons in a fmall way of bufinefs, or of doubtful character in the world : it was carried on by the moft extenfive dealers, and by thofe who poffeffed the faireft reputation. It was carried on too by thofe who avowed, and defended the deed. I am glad they did avow it; for it faves me the unpleafant office of firft mentioning, as I certainly fhould have thought it my duty to do, a practice, which, however fanctified by numbers, I have uniformly

formly condemned and avoided. Nor do I claim any kind of merit in having done so. I avoided the practice, because I thought it wrong: other people adopted it, because they thought it right: and it is well known, that the same act will defervedly be pronounced either good or bad, according to the different laws by which it is tried. Whatever opinion may be formed upon thefe *Laws of the Tea-dealers*, I think it will be univerfally allowed, that *that law of the land*, which leaves every man at liberty to act as he pleafes, and which ferves as a reftraint to thofe, only who are a reftraint to themfelves, no longer anfwers the intentions of thofe who framed it. I have mentioned this circumftance, in order to fhew the inefficacy, and the ftriking perverfion, of the Excife Laws; and I hope no perfon will imagine that I have thus touched upon the practical hiftory of the Tea-dealers, in order to affume credit, or to draw advantage, to myfelf at the expence of others. I repeat, that I am divulging no fecret: and I never defire either credit or advantage, which are to be thus acquired. I am alfo happy to declare, that there are many perfons in the Tea-trade, who have as cordially condemned, and as uniformly fhunned, this practice as myfelf.

It is out of my Province, and, indeed, out of my Power, to enumerate all the evils which attended this deviation from the fpirit of the Eaft India Company's Charter. I will content myfelf with briefly faying, that they were deprived of, at leaft, half their commerce in the important article (important to themfelves at leaft) of Tea: Government

4   was

was defrauded of a confiderable revenue: a very large fum was raifed, moft unequally, and confequently moft unequitably, upon only a part of the confumers of Tea; the fair dealer was oppreffed, and almoft borne down by the Smuggler; and foreign Companies had abfolutely entered into the China Trade, not to fupply the demands of their own country, but to feed our illicit trade.

After this brief, and, I am fure, imperfect catalogue of the evils of Smuggling, I may fairly affign them as the *caufe* of the late Bill: and no perfon, I think, who wifhes well to this country, will deny, that the interference of the legiflature was become highly neceffary, in order to oppofe this great and growing evil.

The *general Intent* of this Bill already appears; it was the fuppreffion of Smuggling; and, thus far at leaft, the intent was commendable. But it is poffible that the object in view might be good, and yet the means of obtaining it, bad: it will therefore be neceffary to confider the *particular means* by which Government *intended* to accomplifh this defirable purpofe.

The high duties upon Tea had, as I have already obferved, afforded a temptation to the Smuggler, which no laws had been able to counteract. Nor did it appear probable, that any, which were confiftent with the mild nature of the Britifh Conftitution, could vanquifh fo formidable an enemy. He was to be deftroyed, not by force of arms, but by the fuppreffion of that gain, which had hitherto encouraged his depredations: and it was reafonable

to

to conclude, that when nothing was to be got by Smuggling, there would be no Smuggler. The enormous duty upon Tea was, then, reduced: and so little was left, that it could by no means make amends for that rifk to which an illicit Trade is liable. Thus far all was well: and thus far every man in the Kingdom, except the Smuggler, was contented. But as the reduction of the Duty upon Tea, of courfe reduced the public revenue; and at a time, when even more money than had hitherto been raifed, was requifite, it became abfolutely neceffary to confider, in what way this deficiency fhould be fupplied. The way which was propofed, and which has been adopted, was, by an additional Duty upon Windows.

In entering upon this part of the fubject, which is certainly the leaft pleafing to myfelf, and probably to the reader, I hope I may be allowed the fmall privilege of beftowing a new Name upon that Bill, which is the object of our prefent confideration. A good Name would be better than precious ointment, and would at leaft cure thofe Complaints, which are, I verily think, to be attributed to the *bad* Name which was given to this Bill upon its firft appearance in the World. Inftead of the *Commutation* Bill, I fhall beg leave to call it the *Tea* Bill. I fhall omit, for the fake of brevity, the other appellation of the Window Bill, to which I confefs it has an equal right.

I do not know the words which Mr. Pitt made ufe of, when he firft opened this Subject in the Houfe of Commons. But if he actually called it
a *Com-*

a *Commutation* Bill, he furely could not mean a *Commutation of perfect pecuniary Equality:* he could not mean, that every man fhould fave precifely as much in the difference of the Price of his Tea, as he would pay for his additional Tax upon Windows. Unlefs the quantities and the prices of Tea, confumed in fimilar Houfes, had been fimilar, fuch a Commutation could not poffibly take place : and he who could believe the promife of fuch a palpable impoffibility, has no right to be fevere upon the Perfon who made it. Indeed, if I were anxious to charge any one with having deceived me, I fhould certainly wifh to bring fome better proof againft him, than his not having performed a promife, which, when it was made, I muft have known it was impoffible for him to perform. Where there could be no deceit, there could be no deceiver. But though the Bill could not be called, in this fenfe of the word, a *Commutation* Bill, yet, in another fenfe, it might lay claim to that Title. It was to commute one Tax for another : and I believe the Public were given to underftand, that the new Tax would be, *upon the whole,* more eligible than the old one, for which it was commuted. They were not to look for perfect pecuniary equality ; but to compare *all* thofe evils which were to be brought on by the new Tax, with thofe which were to be removed by the alteration of the old one. The evil which is brought on by the new Tax is of the pecuniary kind : and, if we confider the fums which are to be paid by individuals of the different claffes which are marked out by the Act, we muft allow it to be a very ferious evil :

B   nor

nor do I wish to make it appear less than it actually is. Some ill consequences which had arisen from the old Tax, and which were therefore to be imputed to it, I have already enumerated. Nor was the pecuniary evil by any means a trivial one. This evil was to be, in a considerable degree, and the other evils were to be almoft completely, removed. Now if for the pecuniary evil of the new Tax, the Public in general were to receive a material, though not a perfectly adequate, pecuniary compenfation; and if the other evils which had already injured, and were likely to injure ftill more, the revenue, the commerce, and the commercial integrity, of this country, were to be completely removed, I really think I might venture to fay, that the Bill would, in that cafe, hold out an advantageous commutation to the Public. This, too, was the commutation which I always thought was intended to be held out; and whatever the Minifter might fay, when this fubject was firft, and, perhaps, fomewhat haftily, mentioned in the Houfe, I am fure that afterwards, when it came to be fully debated, he did exprefsly declare, that this Bill did not promife an exact pecuniary equality.

As far then as I can judge of the *Intent* of this Bill, it was, to fupprefs the Smuggling of Tea, by reducing the duty upon it; and to make good to the Revenue the lofs which this reduction would occafion, by a new duty, which fhould be, *upon the whole*, more eligible than the old one.

Having thus confidered the *Caufe*, and the *Intent*, of the Tea Bill, I fhall now endeavour to

fhew

shew in what respects it has hitherto *failed*, and the *Causes* of that failure.

Of that grand object; the suppression of Smuggling, it is too soon to judge.—The unlawful Tea which was in the kingdom when this Bill passed into a law, was not, by that law, to be annihilated: and the Tea which was upon the continent, and which had been imported thither for the express purpose of supplying this island, was not likely to be averted, even by that reduction of price at which the Bill aimed, from its original destination. The Owners of such Tea would naturally think it more eligible to dispose of their goods at a considerable loss, than not to dispose of them at all. And if the diligence of Smugglers was capable of being encreased, it was likely to be so, for a time, by that act, which threatened their final destruction. I am not therefore alarmed by the temporary prevalence of Smuggling, or elevated by its temporary cessation: But I look forward to the establishment of such moderate prices of Tea in this country, as shall prevent any foreign nation from importing that commodity from China, for our use; perhaps for its own. If, however, the present situation of Smuggling is not to be considered as a criterion by which the merits of the Tea Bill are to be already judged, yet it is a circumstance concerning which the Publick may wish to receive some information. As far as I have been able to learn, Smuggling has already received a very material check; notwithstanding large quantities of Tea are occasionally

landed

'landed upon fome parts of the coaft, and are con-
veyed thence under the protection of very formidable parties of Smugglers.

As a proof that Smuggling has actually received
a material check, I am happy to add, that, as I am
credibly informed, fcarcely any *loofe* Tea (for that
is the appellation which has been beftowed upon
that fmuggled Tea which was fold under the fanc-
tion of a legal Permit) is to be purchafed at this
time, in London.

By faying that even the intended reduction of the
price of Tea would not have given immediate and
complete efficacy to the Tea Bill, I do not mean to
fay, that it was a matter of little confequence, whether the intended reduction took place, at this time,
or not. It is a matter of great confequence to the
ultimate object of this Bill: It is a matter of immediate confequence to thofe perfons, from whom an
additional Window Tax is already exacted; and
nothing fhould have induced me to deliver any
opinion, or any information, upon the prefent fubject, if I had meant to fhrink from this part of the
enquiry. I will endeavour to meet it fairly.—In
order to do fo, I fhall compare thofe average prices
of Tea which were held out before the fale, with
thofe at which the Teas of the laft fale (including
both parts of it), and alfo thofe of the private
trade fale, actually fold.

Average

Average Prices which were held out before the Sale, exclufive of Duty.		Average Prices at which each Species of Tea has actually fold fince the 16th of September, exclufive of Duty.	
	Per lb.		Per lb.
Bohea, —	1 s. 9 d.	——	1 s. 7 d.$\frac{1}{4}$
Congou, —	2 s. 6 d.	——	4 s. 9 d.$\frac{1}{2}$
Souchong, —	3 s. 4 d.	——	6 s. 5 d.$\frac{3}{4}$
Singlo, —	3 s. 4 d.	——	3 s. 5 d.
Hyfon, —	5 s. 8 d.	——	6 s. 8 d.$\frac{1}{4}$

It is right to obferve, that I have not made any Allowance for that excefs of price, which it was certainly reafonable to expect, at the commencement of the new plan. I muft alfo take notice, that when the prices at which the Eaft India Company were expected to fell their Teas, under the new regulation, were firft mentioned, not a word was faid upon the fubject of Difcount: it was therefore reafonable to conclude, that the cuftomary allowance of Difcount would be deducted from thofe prices.

It appears, from this comparative view, that the average price of Bohea Tea is lefs than that which was held out to the Public; and of Singlo, but very little more. With refpect to thefe fpecies of Tea there is, therefore, no caufe of complaint. The excefs in the price of Hyfon Tea is not very confiderable; and when we reflect, that difficulties and unfavourable circumftances ufually accompany great alterations, and that the alteration in the duties upon Tea has had its fhare of them, I fhould hope that this failure in the promifed reduction of the price of Hyfon Tea, would not excite much diffatisfaction; the excefs will, I truft, be of fhort duration.

Of

Of the difficulties to which I have alluded, I
shall shortly take further notice.—The failure in
the reduction of the Prices of Congou and Souchong Teas is considerable indeed : and I confess,
without scruple, that the consumers of these species
of Tea have reason to be extremely dissatisfied.
The reduction in the price of Congou and Souchong certainly does not make any thing like that
pecuniary compensation for the additional Window
Tax, which every man, after making the most liberal
allowance for the difficulties of a new scheme, had
a right to expect. I might, perhaps, venture to
assert, that it would be more advantageous to the
Public to pay 8 *s.* per Pound for their Souchong
Tea as they used to do, if nearly the half of that
sum went into the Public Treasury, than 5 *s.* 8 *d.*
per pound for the same Tea, as they now do,—
when 5 *s.* 0 *d.* 4-9ths are paid to the Company, and
only 7 *d.* 5-9ths for the use of the Public. I have
not mentioned the Tradesman's profit on either
side : he doubtless had it under the old regulation,
and will doubtless expect it under the new.

Though the failure of the Tea Bill, with respect
to the suppression of Smuggling, cannot, from the
present state of that Trade, be ascertained, yet I
do not scruple to declare, that, if the high price
of Congou and Souchong Teas should continue,
there is no doubt but that Smuggling would also
continue; at least there is nothing in the Tea Bill
which could suppress it; and the merit of its being
suppressed by any other Bill, would rather exagge-
rate, than atone for, the failure of suppression by this
Bill.

Bill. If Smuggling could have been fuppreffed, whilft the high prices of Tea continued, there was no neceffity for a Commutation. But this, as I have already faid, was, I believe, impoffible.

It is, then, evident that the Bill has hitherto *failed* to reduce the price of Congou and Souchong Teas fo much, or any thing like fo much, as it ought to have done: and *this* failure has already produced another failure; viz. that of the pecuniary Compenfation which might reafonably have been expected; and unlefs fome proper remedy can be applied, it feems likely to fuperinduce the additional failure of that grand object of the Tea Bill, the Suppreffion of Smuggling.

The *caufes* of this failure are now to be enumerated. It was natural to imagine that the Smuggler, and thofe perfons who had reconciled their confciences to a Trade, which, however unlawful, was extremely profitable, would endeavour, by every ftratagem, to render ineffectual a Bill, of which the avowed intent was, to deftroy their favourite Traffic. The Firft Tea Sale, fubfequent to the alteration of duty, confifted of two parts: in the Firft part were thofe Teas which had been returned by the former purchafers to the Company: in the Second were the new Teas, which were neceffary to complete the quantity contained in the Company's declaration. The commencement of the firft part of this Sale was fuch, as at once aftonifhed and mortified the Fair Dealer, and ftrongly indicated the artful interference of the Smuggler. This fufpicion was, in the courfe of the Sale, repeatedly

peatedly confirmed: nor was it bare fufpicion; for a certain Dealer, who has an undoubted right to be believed when he fays he is well acquainted with the intention of Smugglers, declared, that " Perfons on the other fide of the water, who were poffeffed of Twenty or Thirty thoufand pounds each, were determined to keep up the Prices of Tea; and that they could do fo, notwith-ftanding any oppofition which they might meet with." And I have fince been affured, that the combination which was formed, in order to keep up the prices of Tea at the firft part of the Sale, has been acknowledged by thofe who were con-cerned in it. I will venture then to affert, and I believe every honeft and attentive Tea-dealer will join me in the affertion, that the artful effort of the Smuggler and his abettors, was one caufe of the prefent failure of the Tea Bill.

Nor had the Smuggler, in whom the oppofite qualities of Moloch and Belial are fo happily united, that he is, at all times, equally prepared for War, or for Wiles, a very arduous tafk to perform: for every Tea-dealer whom he met in the Sale-room, was almoft wholly deftitute of Tea. We might, therefore, adopt, fomewhat too readily, thofe prices, which neither our own wants, urgent as they were, had formed, nor our own judgment had approved; but which had been fixed by the artifices of the enemy. And let not the Public be too fevere upon the intemperance of thofe, who after having been reduced to a ftate of famine, had, on a fudden, plenty fet before them. Nor were the Canifters of

the

the Tea-dealers alone without Tea; thofe of almoft every private family in the kingdom had been reduced to their laft leaf; and the fupply for each meal was bought, grudgingly, at the old. price. To the 16th of September, the day upon which the alteration in duty was to take place, the Public looked forward for the promifed and confolatory reduction of the price of Tea: and it was with the utmoft impatience that they fubmitted to the fhort delay, which was neceffary for the fale of that Tea, and for its delivery. The Public, who were thus eager to be fupplied, will, I truft, exercife a little lenity towards the fair dealers who were, perhaps, too eager to fupply them.

Of Souchong and Congou Teas the fcarcity was ftill more extenfive: for the Eaft India Company themfelves had not by any means a fufficient quantity of thofe fpecies in their warehoufes. This circumftance was well known to the Smuggler: and it is not to be fuppofed that he could be apprized of the weaknefs of his adverfary, without taking advantage of it.

The principal caufes of the prefent failure of the Tea Act, and the chief difficulties which accompanied the Tea revolution, were, then, the artifices of the Smuggler, and the fcarcity of Tea throughout the kingdom: not only in the fhop of the Tea-dealer, and in the clofet of the confumer, but alfo in the warehoufes of the Eaft India Company.

These caufes do not entirely agree with thofe which have hitherto been produced to the Public;

C   for

for the prefent failure in the reduction of the price of Tea has repeatedly been attributed to the Minifter, to the Eaft India Company, and the Tea-dealers. With refpect to the Minifter, and the Eaft India Company, it is not my province to enter, at large, into a juftification of the meafures of the one, or of the conduct of the other: they would, of courfe, defpife fo feeble an advocate. But though I fhall not attempt to fay every thing which may be faid upon this fubject, it is neceffary that I fhould fay fomething.—The Tea Act held out to the Public certain prices, at or near which, each fpecies of Tea was expected to be fold under the new regulation: and the Act alfo contained claufes, which were exprefly calculated to prevent any material deviation from thofe prices. The Eaft India Company were to keep " a ftock of " Tea, at leaft equal to one year's confumption, " according to the fales of the preceding year, " always beforehand: They were to make, at the " leaft, four fales in every year. They were to ex- " pofe to publick fale, at the leaft, five millions of " pounds weight of Tea," at the Firft Sale; and to put up, at the leaft, two millions and a half at the Second Sale. Thus were the Eaft India Company obliged to put up at their two firft Sales, a larger quantity of Tea than they had ufually delivered in twelve months; and a larger quantity than the confumption, both legal and illegal, of fix months, had, according to the moft probable calculations, ever been.

The

The prices at which each fpecies of Tea was to be put up at the four firft fales were not to exceed thofe mentioned in the Act. Provifion was alfo made for a regular Importation of Tea; and for its never being expofed to fale at higher prices than thofe which it actually coft the Company. That all thefe cautions fhould immediately produce their full effect, and that the average prices of the Tea which was to be fold at the firft fale, fhould not at all exceed thofe at which the Plan aimed, was more, I believe, than Mr. Pitt promifed, or than the Dealers in Tea expected: but I alfo believe that both Mr. Pitt and the Dealers in Tea did expect, that the excefs of Price would have been inconfiderable; and confequently lefs, very far lefs, than it has actually been, with refpect to Congou and Souchong Teas. I own that I did not expect fuch a failure myfelf: nor can I, after the moft cool and impartial examination of what has paft, find any reafon to condemn myfelf for not having expected it.

The Eaft India Directors appear to me to have done every thing in their power, after the Bill had paffed, to give efficacy to the plan, and to infure thofe reduced prices of Tea which it promifed. Inftead of putting up barely five millions of Tea at the firft Sale, as they were bound to do, they put up nearly fix millions and a quarter: nor was this all; for they put up fome fpecies of Tea, at lower prices than thofe which were mentioned in the Act. So that, inftead of adhering ftrictly to the quantity and to the prices which the Tea Act

would

would have warranted, they made a deviation with refpect to each, in favour of the Public.

But notwithftanding all this, the Directors who prefided at the Sale, faw, I hope with regret, immoderate prices given for fome fpecies of Tea, and too much for others. To reftrain this evil was, however, out of their power; and they might as well have faid to the raging waves of the ocean, as to the defigning Tea-buyer, " Thus far fhalt " thou come, and no further." Nay more, the Directors, at the requeft of the fair dealers in Tea, fufpended the Sale, and adopted the advice of thofe dealers, in order to reduce, if poffible, the prices which had been given at the beginning of the Sale.

It is, I think, fair to obferve, in this place, that though I really think the Eaft India Directors have thus endeavoured to prevent the prefent high prices of Tea, yet I do not mean to affert that they are therefore entitled to any peculiar degree of praife. The Tea Act certainly promifed confiderable advantages to the Eaft India Company: but all thefe advantages depended upon a reduction of price. To endeavour then to put a ftop to thofe high prices, which were utterly incompatible with the fpirit of the new regulation, was at once the intereft and the duty of the Eaft India Company. This part of their duty had been recently and exprefsly pointed out in the following words of the Act: " And whereas it is juft and reafonable that " the faid United Company fhould, in confide- " ration of the great *benefit* which may refult to
" their

" their commerce from the reduction of duties
" hereby made, contribute their utmoft endea-
" vours for fecuring to the Public the full benefit
" which will arife from an *immediate* and perma-
" nent reduction of prices, &c."

Of the conduct of the Tea-dealers it is my peculiar province to fpeak : they have been blamed,
they have been accufed, moft feverely and unde-
fervedly ; and common juftice requires that fome
perfon fhould ftand up in their defence. This
office has fallen upon me. I wifh for their fake,
as well as my own, that they had found an abler
advocate.

I am aware that when a Tea-dealer pleads the
caufe of Tea-dealers, his impartiality is likely to be
fufpected ; but whatever attachment I have to
them, I hope I have a ftill ftronger attachment to
Truth ; and if I did not know that they merited
defence, I would not attempt to defend them.

The reader will, I hope, pardon me, if I give
a fhort hiftory of the conduct of the Tea-dealers,
relative to the Tea Bill. We have not been accuftomed to obtrude ourfelves upon the publick
notice ; and having once told our plain and artlefs
tale, we fhall cheerfully leave our caufe to the
judgment of the Public, and retire ; confident of
our own integrity and of their candour.

The Tea-dealers had long beheld the alarming
increafe of Smuggling ; and they had found, that
every reftraint, even the beft which they themfelves
could recommend, had proved ineffectual : for no
fooner was one head fevered from this monfter,

than

than another fprouted up in its place. The purchafe of loofe Tea was, at firft, confined to a few
dealers : but when it appeared that they carried on
their trade with perfect fecurity, and that, by
having difcovered a cheaper market than that of
the Eaft India Company, they were underfelling
the fair Trader, and obliging him to facrifice
either his juft profit, or his trade, the number of
thefe purchafers encreafed : and at length many
perfons who had ftrenuoufly oppofed, and zealoufly
endeavoured to deftroy, this commerce of art,
openly, and yet reluctantly, engaged in it.

A Committee of Tea-dealers had been eftablifhed
fome years, in order to watch and counteract the
fchemes of the Smuggler : and the Eaft India
Company very liberally agreed to fubfcribe 500l.
towards the expences of this Society, I need not
make any apology to the reader for declining to
give him the detail of our deliberations : we took
great pains to little purpofe, and were at laft obliged
to confefs, that the children of this world were too
wife for us.

It was, I think, during the Seffions of Parliament before the laft, that we were roufed from our
ftate of defpair, by being told that a plan was in
agitation, for the reduction of the duties upon
Tea; and we underftood that this plan had been
prefented to the Minifter by the Eaft India Company, and was favourably received. A Committee
was alfo appointed by the Houfe of Commons to
enquire into the ftate of Smuggling; and as we
had reafon to think that an application from the

Tea-

Tea-dealers to this Committee, might be of ser-
vice, we delivered in a plan similar, or nearly similar, to that which had been delivered to the Minister by the East India Company : making, at the
same time, a few remarks upon the subject. I do
not know that any conference, relative to this busi-
ness, was held between the Duke of Portland (who,
if I am not mistaken, was the Minister at that
time) and the Dealers in Tea: or that any an-
swer was given to the plan which had been delivered to the Committee of the House of Commons: but the general expectation of the Tea-
dealers was, that some alteration would, ere long,
take place in the duty upon Tea. The information
which we were able to obtain at the India House
warranted this expectation; and the subsequent
publication of the Reports from the Committee
helped to confirm it.

The change in the Ministry, though it threatened
an interruption of any plan of alteration which
might have been formed, by no means destroyed
our hopes. It seemed to be generally allowed, by
all parties, that it was become highly necessary to
put a stop to, or, at least to reduce within moderate bounds, this pernicious practice of Smuggling:
and we trusted, that, whichever party prevailed, a
scheme of evident utility, would not be abandoned.

In this state of uncertainty, in which hope prevailed, we entered the Sale-room at the East
India House in May, 1784. The sale consisted of
a very large quantity of Tea; and it was certainly
reasonable that those persons who were to be the
buyers

buyers of it, fhould know, whether any alteration in the duty upon Tea was to take place, or not, before the goods which were then offered to fale fhould be difpofed of. As the Directors, who are prefent at the Sales, attend for the fole purpofe of regulating them, and are not authorized to anfwer queftions of importance, in the name of the Court of Directors, I took care to give proper notice to the Gentlemen in the Direction, on the day previous to the Sale, of the queftion which would be afked at the commencement of it, relative to the expected alteration of the duty upon Tea. At the commencement of the Sale, the queftion was accordingly afked; and the anfwer given was, as nearly as I can recollect it, " That no converfation had lately taken place upon that fubject between the Minifter and the Directors; that they had no reafon to expect any alteration in Duty at any particular time; but that whenever this bufinefs fhould be agitated, we might be affured that the Gentlemen in the Direction would pay a proper attention to the intereft of the Holders of Tea." We thought it was out of the power of the Directors to fay more: we were, therefore, fatisfied with their anfwer, and the Sale began.

At this Sale the Dealers in Tea were to provide themfelves with Goods for the confumption of fix months: the ufual diftance of one Sale from another. And this was done as nearly as, in general, it had been done. Some perfons might buy rather more than their confumption; fome rather lefs: but there was no material fpeculation: and the

4   prices

prices given at this Sale, were the fair prices, which were juftified by the circumftances of the Trade.

The Sale was fcarcely over, when the Tea-dealers, who were of courfe loaded with Goods, heard that a Bill was to be brought into Parliament, almoft immediately, in order to leffen the duty upon Tea. A Meeting of the Trade was called; and a Committee was then appointed in order to wait upon the Minifter, and the Eaft India Directors, and to take fuch other fteps as they might think neceffary.

And here I crave the attention of the Public—whom I am forry to trouble with fo long a hiftory—to the requifition of the Tea-dealers. They required that the intended Plan, which, they confeffed, promifed to be productive of Advantage to themfelves, might not, at the outfet, fubject them to a heavy and ruinous lofs. Every wifh of gain they exprefsly difclaimed. This requifition was, indeed, allowed, by all parties, to be perfectly fair: the only Queftion was, in what manner it was to be complied with. The Modes which were pointed out by the Dealers in Tea were two: Firft, that the Eaft India Company fhould take back their Teas at prime Coft: or, Secondly, that a fufficient time fhould be allowed to the Dealers to difpofe of their Stock, before any alteration in the Duty fhould take place. After repeated Meetings and repeated Deliberations, the Eaft India Directors, who, when the idea of their taking back the Tea at prime coft was firft mentioned, feemed to think it impracticable, fent the following Paper to the Committee of Tea-dealers.

D   " At

" At a Court of Directors, the 4th of
" Auguft, 1784.

" There is in agitation a general Plan for carry-
" ing more effectually into execution the prevent-
" ing of Smuggling of Tea. In this plan the re-
" lief of the former purchafers of Tea at our fales
" (under the alterations which may take place)
" forms a part. In order to bring the whole plan
" to maturity, it is fubmitted to the confideration
" of the Dealers in Tea, whofe general fentiments
" the Court wifhes to know, whether it will be
" a fufficient relief to them to receive back the
" compleat lots of uncleared Teas in the Com-
" pany's Warehoufes at the prices they paid for
" them, upon receiving certificates from the Com-
" pany, which fhall be taken as cafh at their future
" fale, or if not paid in at the next prompt, then
" to be payable at the Company's Treafury on
" demand."

The Committee immediately called a general
Meeting of the Trade; by whom the following
Anfwer was given to the Directors.

" At a General Meeting of the Dealers in
" Tea, held at the New York Coffee Houfe,
" on Thurfday, Auguft 5th, 1784.

" The propofition of the Directors of the Eaft
" India Company being taken into confideration,
" it is unanimoufly agreed by the Holders of Tea
" prefent at this meeting, that with refpect to their
" Teas in the Eaft India Company's warehoufes,
" they

" they are ready to return them to the East India
" Company at prime coft; the Company being at
" liberty to reject the remaining parts of thofe
" lots, of which any part fhall have been cleared
" after the 5th of Auguft. And the Dealers in
" Tea will cheerfully give to Government, to the
" Eaft India Company, and to the Public in ge-
" neral, this proof, that it is by no means their
" Wifh to reap any advantage from the Stock of
" Teas, which they now hold in the Eaft India
" Company's warehoufes."

It was, at the fame time, declared to be underftood by the Dealers in Tea, that the propofal of
the Eaft India Company fhould not affect the Teas
which were in their own fhops, and had paid all
the duties ; but that the time which the Dealers
had reafon to think was intended to be allowed
them for the difpofal of thofe Teas, before the
Eaft India Company had made this propofal,
fhould ftill be allowed.

As to the requifition of the Dealers, refpecting
thofe Teas in their own warehoufes, which had
paid the full duties, the Public will, I truft, immediately fee, that it was fair and equitable.
Thofe Teas had paid duties which amounted nearly
to cent. per cent.; and fuddenly to have reduced
the value of thofe Teas, fo confiderably as the
plan propofed to do, would have been an act of
the moft flagrant injuftice ; and would completely
have ruined, no inconfiderable number of the fair
Tea-dealers in this kingdom.

To the Anfwer of the Tea-dealers, the following
reply was made by the Eaft India Directors.

" At

" At a Court of Directors of the United
" East India Company, the 6th August,
" 1784.

" The Court refumed the confideration of a pro-
" pofal received yefterday from the Committee of
" Tea-dealers, figned by Mr. Twining their Chair-
" man, and thereon refolved, That this Court doth
" accept the faid propofal on the following con-
" ditions; viz. That, from this day forward, none
" of the Tea now uncleared fhall be delivered to
" the Buyers, except in whole lots, or in the
" whole of what this day remains of any broken
" lot or lots.

" And that this Court will forthwith, upon the
" commencement of the new duty, grant to each
" Proprietor of Tea then remaining uncleared in
" the Company's warehoufes, a certificate for the
" fum of money he fhall have paid the Company
" for the fame; which certificate fhall be taken as
" cafh at the next Tea Sale, or if not fo paid in,
" fhall be paid in cafh, upon demand, at any time
" after the next prompt."

Of the two propofals which had, at the commencement of this bufinefs, been made by the
Tea-dealers, that of returning their Teas to the
Eaft India Company was then at length adopted.
It is not neceffary to give a circumftantial account
of what paffed relative to the other propofal; viz.
that of allowing the Dealers a fufficient time for
the difpofal of their goods: I will only briefly obferve,

serve, that the Tea-dealers voluntarily made an offer, upon a suppofition that the Teas were not to be returned, which would, according to the expected prices of the new Teas, have fubjected them to a confiderable lofs.

The propofal which had been adopted by the Eaft India Company, had alfo the Minifter's preference: and, as I underftood, for this reafon; that the reduction of duty would, according to this plan, take place much fooner than it could do according to the other. And fo enormous was the influx of illicit Tea at that time, and fo fpirited were the exertions of the Smuggler, that it was certainly defirable to bring forward, as fpeedily as poffible, that law, by which he was to be controuled.

I readily confefs, that I frequently mentioned to Mr. Pitt this plan of returning the Tea, as one which was, in itfelf, perfectly fair: which would be fatisfactory to the dealers in Tea; and alfo advantageous to the Public. It certainly was fair: and as it exempted the holders of Tea from all lofs, which was the utmoft they ever required, it ought to be, to thofe holders, fatisfactory. As one of them, I have ever been thoroughly fatiffied. But to the Public, it did not prove advantageous. For if, when we entered the fale room in September, we had been in poffeffion of thofe Teas which we returned, and had not been, as we were, under the neceffity of becoming purchafers at the firft part of the fale, the Smugglers could not, even with all their cunning, and all their

their wealth, have raifed the Tea to thofe prices at
which it has actually fold. We could, in that
cafe, have permitted the Smuggler to have been
not only a bidder upon every lot, but alfo a buyer
of every lot: till we had, at length, feen him
buried, like Samfon, under the cumbrous load
which he had heaped upon himfelf. As it was,
we could not poffibly exercife this forbearance;
we had multitudes of orders; and if we meant to
execute them, and to be Tea-dealers, it was certainly neceffary that we fhould purchafe Tea.
Thus were we reduced, in a confiderable degree,
to the Smuggler's mercy—a dreadful fituation for
a fair trader!—and by that very circumftance
which we thought would have haftened his over-
throw.—If I had forefeen that this evil confequence was likely to arife from our propofal of
returning the Teas, I certainly would have mentioned it to Mr. Pitt. Perhaps I ought to have
forefeen it. However this may be, I will never
decline acknowledging any part which I may have
taken, becaufe it has not fully anfwered my expectation: and, in the prefent inftance, a practical
Tea-dealer was certainly more culpable for want
of forefight, than the Minifter.

It fhould however be remembered, that when I
mentioned the plan of returning our Teas to the Eaft
India Company at prime coft, as a plan which was
likely to be advantageous to the Public, the Dealers
in Tea were affured, and they believed, that the
fame Teas would be refold to the Public, at lower
prices than thofe at which they were returned.

The

The Directors themselves, who made the proposal of taking back our Tea at prime coft, declared that they expected to be confiderable lofers by fo doing: but that they were willing to fubmit to this lofs, becaufe they were convinced it would be advantageous to the Public, to have the new Act take place as fpeedily as poffible. That there could be no deceit on the part of the Tea-dealers, is, I think, moft apparent: for if they could have forefeen that their Teas would be worth much more money under the new regulation, than they were under the old, (and we had been repeatedly affured that if we kept the Teas, we fhould not pay more than the new duty upon them), we certainly fhould not have been fo anxious to have returned thofe Teas at prime coft. I do not mean to imply that the Directors expected that profit, which they have actually received upon the returned Teas. I will not think fo ill of them as to fuppofe they did expect it.

I have now given a circumftantial and true, but, I fear, tedious account of the conduct of the Tea-dealers, previous to the commencement of the firft part of the September fale. This fale had fcarcely commenced, when we faw that fuch prices were actually giving for Teas, as foreboded a total defeat of the plan. The fale, however, was undoubtedly open to the difhoneft as well as to the honeft bidder; and it was in this cafe, as it is in many others, far more difficult to correct the evil, than to difcover it's caufe. The Committee who had been appointed by the Dealers in general to

4   act

act for them throughout the whole of this busineſs; held a momentary conſultation in the ſale room; and agreed, in conſequence of it, to requeſt that the ſale might be, for a ſhort time at leaſt, ſuſpended; in order to give the Committee an opportunity of trying, if they could deviſe, ere it was too late, any plan, which might put a ſtop to ſuch prices as were incompatible with the promiſes and the intent of the Tea Act. This requeſt of ſuſpending the ſale was readily complied with by the Director who was preſent: and I am happy to add, that the meaſures which were recommended by the Committee of Tea-dealers, were adopted, in the handſomeſt manner, by the Court of Directors: They made every declaration which we wiſhed them to make; and they permitted the purchaſers of thoſe Teas which had been already bought at this ſale, to relinquiſh their purchaſes. I do not know that it was in the power of the Directors to do more than this: and if they had been inclined to avail themſelves of ſuch a plea, I queſtion whether they could have found a precedent for doing ſo much.

Though our effort was not attended with perfect ſucceſs, and though we had ſtill the old enemy, and our other difficulties, to ſtruggle with, yet we had clearly done ſome good; and Teas ſold more reaſonably than they had done.

The ſale went on with but little, if any, interruption, till we came to the Souchong and Congou Teas: and here our ſurprize and our fears were greater than ever. Here we found that the Smuggler

gler was labouring with all his might; and not without reafon: for it was upon thefe fpecies of Tea that his hopes principally depended. The Committee of Tea-dealers once more defired that the fale might be fufpended: and they made fuch requefts to the Directors, as they thought would be moft likely to lower the prices of Congou and Souchong Teas. Our requefts were partly complied with: and the refult of this fecond fufpenfion bore fome refemblance to that of the firft. We certainly did good: and we had, befides, the fatiffaction of thinking, that we had done *all* the good which it was in our power to do.

One very important point, refpecting the Tea-dealers, remains to be confidered; and I own, without the leaft hefitation, that if they fhould be found faulty in this, the former part of their conduct, however blamelefs, or even however meritorious, cannot be pleaded, for one inftant, in their defence. The point to which I allude, is, not only how they *bought* their Teas, but how they *fold* them to the Public.

And here I have feen the utmoft mifreprefentation; iffuing too from thofe quarters, whence I fhould leaft have expected it. The charge is ferious: it affects a numerous body of Men, and therefore ought not to have been lightly advanced: efpecially by thofe perfons, who knew that what they advanced was likely to be credited.

To mention the precife profit which every Tea-dealer gets, upon every article which he fells, is, of courfe, out of my power. It is not, however,

E

out of my power to mention the rule of conduct
which I myself have followed: and if it should
be thought right, I can only say, that I believe it
has been the conduct of the Tea-dealers in general. Should it be thought wrong, I wish the Tea-
dealers to avow a better rule: that whilst I am suf-
fering the punishment which may be due to my
own sins, I may at least have the satisfaction of
saying,

" Nec quemquam nostri, nisi me, læsere libelli."

Upon the delivery of the new Teas, I arranged
them into different sorts, corresponding, as nearly
as possible, to the qualities of the different sorts
of Tea which we sold under the old regulation.
Having thus fixed the qualities, it remained to fix
the prices: and this I did, by adding to the prime
cost of each article, what I thought a reasonable
profit. This, I confess, I added; and this, I confess, I always will add. There are, indeed, persons
in our trade, as well as in almost every other, who
are constantly selling *at* or *under* prime cost. Such
persons I have ever considered either as fools or
impostors, and I will neither imitate nor deal with
them. When a reasonable profit no longer attends
trade, I will quit it. I believe every body will allow that it was our duty not to add an exorbitant profit. Will they not also allow, that it was
our interest not to do it?—The Tea Trade had
undergone a great revolution (if I may once more
apply such an important word to such an unimportant subject), and it behoved every man to be dili-
gent,

gent, not only to keep his old cuftomers, but alfo to get new ones: not to get them by mean and paltry artifices, from other tradefmen as honeft as himfelf, but to get them from thofe Smugglers and their abettors, who would not, it was to be hoped, be any longer able to fupply them. Now the man who, at fuch a time, afked an exorbitant price for his goods, not only negleted, what is too often negleted, his duty; but he alfo negleted, what is feldom negleted, his intereft.—If any one fhould here be inclined to afk—What *is* your profit? I reply at once, that I will not tell him: and for two reafons: one is, that I think no perfon has a right to claim from a tradefman an anfwer to fuch a queftion: the other is, that he who will not believe me, when I tell him that my profit is no more than is reafonable, will not believe me when I tell him, what that profit actually is.

I concluded my remarks upon the conduct of the Eaft India Directors, with obferving, that though they had performed their duty, by endeavouring to keep down the price of Teas, yet they were not, upon that account, entitled to any particular degree of praife: becaufe, whilft they had been performing their duty, they had been promoting their intereft. When I introduced this remark, I fully intended to make a fimilar obfervation upon the conduct of the Tea-dealers: for to their conduct it is equally applicable.

In this Hiftory of the Tea-dealers, I fhall venture to infert, by way of epifode (and I truft there is a fufficient connection to juftify my doing fo), a

E 2   fair

fair account of thofe Teas, with which the Public
have been fupplied, fince the alteration of duty.

I will not attempt the Augean labour of bring-
ing forth that mafs of flander, with which fome
perfons have endeavoured to contaminate the
Teas of the firft part of the laft Sale. How
often have they been reprefented as the fweepings
of the Eaft India Company's warehoufes! As the
moft execrable ftuff with which the palates of the
Public were ever infulted! And as if all this were
not enough, fome perfon has had the great good-
nefs to caution the unwary, and to inform them,
that no Tea was to be bought, except fuch as was
adulterated, or was mixed with the pernicious manufacture of this country. In fhort, that innocent
and amufing ftream of flander, for which the Tea-
table has long been celebrated, feems of late to
have fwelled into a furious torrent, and to have
endangered even the Tea-table itfelf.—But the late
Act of Parliament, which commuted one Tax for another, certainly *could* not alter the intrinfic quality
of every cheft of Tea in the Eaft India Company's
warehoufes; and I hope *did* not convert every Tea-
dealer in the Kingdom into a rafcal. I fhall be very
glad to fee that it is in the power of the Legiflature
to make all the Tea-dealers in the Kingdom honeft:
it is not in its power to make them all difhoneft.

It was my intention to give, in this place, a
circumftantial account of the importation of thofe
teas, which have already been expofed to Sale,
fince the 16th of September: but as fuch an
account appears in the Eaft India Company's
Report,

Report, I may of courfe fupprefs mine. It appears from the Appendix, No. 2. of that Report, that a very few chefts of Tea had lain in the Eaft India Company's warehoufes a confiderable length of time. The fact is, they had loft their owners: and were in a fituation fimilar to that of the unclaimed Stock at the Bank. By the late Act of Parliament, which made an alteration in the duty upon Tea, it was enacted, That *all* the Teas which fhould be in the Eaft India Company's warehoufes on the 15th of September, fhould become the property of the Company. The unclaimed Tea was therefore become their own, and was once more put up to Sale.—As the Teas which had been fold prior to the year 1781, were liable to have fuftained fome injury, and as a very few chefts of each fpecies had remained in the warehoufes a moft unufual length of time, all thofe Teas were again expofed to view: and, whatever fome people may imagine, they had not, even in the courfe of fo many years, changed their nature. We found that they were ftill Teas: affected indeed by age: but they were valued, not according to their paft, but according to their prefent, qualities.

The Teas which formed the fecond part of the firft Sale, and the Teas of the private Trade Sale, were certainly frefher and better than the returned Teas in the former part of the firft Sale: but this is no more than is ufual:—the Teas of the lateft importation ought ever to have the advantage; and there is, at this time, a very large quantity of frefh and good Teas in the poffeffion of the Dealers.

There

There are two other charges which have been brought, with vaſt induſtry, and vaſt appearance of regard for the Public, againſt the Teas with which they have been lately ſupplied. The Charges to which I allude, are thoſe of *mixing* and *adulterating* Teas. I ſhall beg leave to conſider theſe accuſations ſeparately, notwithſtanding they have been ſo artfully blended together.

If the mixing of Tea is a crime, and an impoſition upon the Public, I readily confeſs that I have a multitude of crimes and impoſitions to anſwer for; and that my good Father and Grandfather little merited thoſe fair Charaĉters which they left behind them, and for which I have ever reſpeĉted their Memories. I will make to the Public a family confeſſion, and I hope I ſhall obtain from the Public a family abſolution.

In my Grandfather's time—for it is a tale to which I have often willingly attended, whatever the reader may do—it was the cuſtom for Ladies and Gentlemen to come to the ſhop, and to order their own Teas—The cheſts uſed to be ſpread out, and when my Grandfather had mixed ſome of them together, *in the preſence of his cuſtomers*, they uſed to taſte the Tea: and the mixing was varied till it ſuited the palates of the purchaſers. At that time of day, no perſon would have liked the Tea, if it had not been mixed. The cuſtom of the purchaſers taſting Tea in this manner was ſeldom practiſed in my Father's time: now, it is ſcarcely ever practiſed: but the old cuſtom of mixing Teas has been uniformly continued: and if I muſt now lay it aſide, I can

only

only fay, that I have been learning a leffon, which is not very eafily learned, to little purpofe. I think however that the cuftom only requires proper explanation to be approved. Throw off the veil of myftery, and many things which were before alarming, appear to be perfectly harmlefs.

Whoever underftands Tea, and clears home, for example, twenty Chefts of Hyfon, will find, upon tafting them feparately and accurately, that fome have rather too much flavor, and are therefore coarfe, fome have too little, and are therefore weak; and that others have—perhaps like thofe who are to drink them—fome little peculiarity, which a proper union will totally remove. By making a judicious mixture out of thefe Chefts, a better Tea may be got, than any of the Chefts, taken fingly, could afford. Befides, if this cuftom were not to be practifed, it would be impoffible to preferve that fimilarity of Tea, at any given price, which every Dealer muft preferve, if he means to give fatisfaction to his cuftomer. The pound of Tea which he bought out of one of the twenty Chefts to-day, might perhaps be approved: but if he comes to-morrow, that Cheft may be gone, and another neither is, nor of courfe can, without mixing, be made like it. As to impofition, if the Tea, when mixed, be good, and honeftly worth the price which is required for it, who is impofed upon? Who will complain? If the Tea, though taken out of a fingle Cheft, be not good, and not worth the money which is afked for it, will not every perfon think himfelf impofed upon? Will not every perfon complain?

complain? I hope then that the Tea-dealer who fairly and anxiously mixes his Chests of genuine Tea together, in order, not to impose upon his customers, but to give them satisfaction, will no longer be ranked with the adulterators of Tea.

I have confined myself to the Instance of my own practice, because I have no right to speak with equal freedom, and equal certainty, of the practice of others: so far however from intending to lay claim to the sole possession of the art of mixing, I verily believe it is, and always was, generally practised. There is indeed one species of Tea— I mean Bloom—which though it actually improves other Teas, when properly mixed with them, would, by itself, be almost universally disliked. If, after all, any person should prefer his own opinion in this matter to that of the Tea-dealers, and would be better pleased with his Tea, if it came out of a single chest, than if it were mixed, he may certainly have it so. We shall not offer, like the fifty Patriotic Gentlemen, who threatened to open Tea-shops, in order to prevent the imposition of the present Tea-dealers, to *swear* that it is not mixed; because when we say it, we hope we shall be believed. Nor can we expect that any person will enter our shops to buy a pound of Tea, if he should think it necessary to guard the purchase with an oath.

There are, it seems, persons, who have bought Tea for the express purpose of critically inspecting it; and who have industriously declared, upon such an inspection, that they discovered, even in

one

one half pound of Tea, three or four different forts
of leaves; and have, upon this difcovery, grounded
an accufation both againft Tea and Tea-dealers.
Of thefe perfons I muft obferve, that like all who
fet themfelves up for critics in a matter which they
do not underftand, they difplay much more zeal
than judgment. I fhall prefume to inform thefe
infpectors, that in every cheft of Tea a diffimilarity
of leaf may be difcovered. Perhaps thefe Gentlemen imagine that the leaves which are contained
in any one cheft, grew, in China, upon the fame
tree. But if they did, they would ftill vary in
appearance: and, in that cafe, the variation fhould
be attributed, not to the Tea-dealer, but to the
principles of vegetation; by which the leaves
upon a fingle tree will often exhibit a variety of
tints.

I do not however mean to deny, that the Tea in
queftion was mixed. I only wifh to fhew the ab-
furdity of that mode by which the mixture is to be
proved, and in confequence of which, the Tea is
to be condemned.

The other accufation, viz. that of adulterating
Teas, does, indeed, deferve the public attention :
and I fhall give the Public the beft information in
my power concerning it.

It is well known, that very large quantities of
leaves are manufactured in this Ifland, for the ex-
prefs purpofe of adulterating Teas: fuch a mixture,
I fhall, without fcruple, call Adulteration. Thefe
leaves are prepared in various ways, in order to

F   fuit

fuit the various kinds of Tea, which they are intended to adulterate.

I fhall here communicate to the Public a particular account of this manufacture, which I have lately received from a Gentleman, who has made very accurate enquiries relative to this fubject.

" *Method of making* Smouch *with Afh Tree leaves, to mix with Black Teas.*

" When gathered they are firft dried in the fun, then baked, they are next put upon a floor and trod upon until the leaves are fmall, then fifted and fteeped in copperas, with fheeps dung ; after which being dried on a floor, they are fit for ufe."

Another Mode.

" When the leaves are gathered they are boiled in a copper with copperas and fheeps dung ; when the liquor is ftrained off, they are baked and trod upon, until the leaves are fmall, after which they are fit for ufe.

" The quantity manufactured at a fmall village, and within eight or ten miles thereof, cannot be afcertained ; but is fuppofed to be about Twenty Tons in a year.—One man acknowledges to have made Six hundred weight in every week, for fix months together.

The fine is fold at 4*l*. 4*s*. per Cwt. equal to 9*d*. per lb. The coarfe,   2*l*. 2*s*. ditto,   ditto,   4¼*d*. ditto.

" Elder buds are manufactured in fome places, to reprefent fine Teas."

This

This iniquitous trade has been carried on a long time: though not in fo extenfive a way as within thefe few years. In the 11th Geo. I. cap. 30, fect. 5, it is enacted, " That the Dealer in Tea, or Manufacturer, or Dyer thereof, who fhall counterfeit or adulterate Tea, or fhall alter, fabricate, or manufacture it with *Terra Japanica*, or with any other drug or drugs whatfoever, or fhall mix with Tea any leaves, other than leaves of Tea, [thus, in the time of Geo. I. real Tea was allowed to be mixed with real Tea], or other ingredients whatfoever, fhall forfeit the fum of One hundred pounds."

It is alfo recited, in the 4th of Geo. II. cap. 14, fect. 11, " That feveral ill difpofed perfons do frequently dye, fabricate, or manufacture, very great quantities of Sloe leaves, Liquorifh leaves, and the leaves of Tea that have before been ufed, or the leaves of other trees, fhrubs, or plants, in imitation of Tea, and do likewife mix, colour, ftain, and dye, fuch leaves, and likewife Tea, with Terra Japanica, Sugar, Moloffes, Clay, Logwood, and with other ingredients, and do fell and vend the fame as true and real Tea, to the prejudice of the health of his Majefty's fubjects, the diminution of the Revenue, and to the ruin of the Fair Trader:" and the dealer in, or feller of, fuch " *fophifticated*" Tea, is to forfeit the fum of Ten pounds for every pound weight.

It appears from the 17th of Geo. III. cap. 29, That this trade had increafed to a very great degree, " to the injury and deftruction of great quantities of

" timber,

" timber, woods, and underwoods, the prejudice of
" the health of his Majefty's fubjects, the diminution
" of the revenue, the ruin of the fair trader, and to
" the encouragement of idlenefs:" and, by the fame
act, the feller or manufacturer of fuch Tea is to
forfeit Five pounds per pound weight; or upon
nonpayment of that fum, be committed to prifon,
for any time not exceeding twelve months.

Hitherto Government has not been able to fupprefs this trade: but, when the fmuggling of real
Tea fhall claim lefs of their attention, I hope they
will exert themfelves with vigour, and put a ftop to
the manufacture of Englifh Tea.

It is, then, fufficiently apparent, that there is
fuch a thing as adulterated Tea: there is plenty of
it: and the Public may naturally enquire how they
are to avoid it. My anfwer is, By buying their
Tea of reputable Tea-dealers, who are, I dare fay,
to be found in every part of the kingdom; and
by avoiding thofe dealers of a different defcription,
who offer their Teas to fale at lower prices than
thofe at which legal and genuine Teas can be
afforded. I will take this opportunity of declaring,
that whenever I mention Tea-dealers, I never mean
to include thofe perfons, who, notwithftanding
they fell Tea, are more properly claffed with another defcription of men, of whom I have had frequent occafion to fpeak.

I will now clofe the hiftory of the Tea-dealers:
and I will leave the Public to judge, whether the
prefent failure in the reduction of the price of Tea
to the confumer, is owing to thofe caufes which
I have

I have affigned; viz. to the artifices of the Smuggler, and the general fcarcity of Tea ; or whether
it ought to be attributed to the Minifter, the Eaft
India Company, or the Tea-dealer.

Having thus endeavoured to fhew the original
Caufe, and alfo the *Intent* of the Tea Act ; and the
refpects in which it has *failed*, with the caufes of
that failure, it remains for me to point out thofe
methods, which are moft likely to *correct* it ; to
remove the *principal objections* that are made to this
act ; and to render it productive of thofe *good purpofes* for which it was framed.

I have hitherto proceeded with fome degree of
confidence, becaufe I have feldom quitted the firm
ground of matter of fact. I come now to the fal-
lible furface of my own opinion, and my own con-
jecture; and I fhall advance, as I ought to do,
with caution and timidity.

It may perhaps be thought, that I fhould have
contented myfelf with pointing out the evil, and
modeftly have confefled, that I muft leave the
cure of it to others. But fuch modefty is, too
often, allied to vanity : and whatever men may
fay, I believe they ufually think, that a conftant
attention to any particular profeffion, enables them
to form fome opinion, relative to it. Upon the
prefent fubject I will at leaft venture to give my
opinion ; and I wifh it to be confidered as the *blot* of
an unfkilful artift, which may be worked up, by
fuperior abilities, to fome degree of perfection.

Whoever attempts to correct the prefent failure
in the Tea Bill, ought to confider, who are the
fufferers

sufferers by that failure: and they are undoubtedly the Public. I think I may venture to assert, that it is no small consolation to Government, if the failure of any plan which it forms, be accompanied with an increase of revenue. In the present instance, the failure has not only been accompanied with, but has actually been the cause of, a very considerable increase. For as the new duty upon Tea, of 12 and a half per cent., is an ad valorem duty, Government has of course received a much larger sum for duties upon the Teas of last sale, than it would have done if they had sold at the expected prices.

The consolatory sum which the East India Company have received from the failure in the proposed reduction of the price of Tea, is enormous indeed.—Upon the first part of the sale, which consisted of the returned Teas, they gained about 64,000*l*: they declared that they expected to be considerable losers by those Teas: and I believe I may venture to say, that the sum produced by the first part of the sale only, exceeded that which the Company originally expected it would produce, about One Hundred Thousand Pounds.

In order to give some idea of the whole of that additional and consolatory sum, which, in consequence of a failure in the reduction of price, has already been paid by the Public to the East India Company, and the owners of the private trade Teas, I will shew, what the amount of those Teas has actually been, exclusive of duty; and what it would have been, if each species of Tea had sold

at

at that price, at which the Company faid they were willing to fell it.

	£.
The Eaft India Company, and their Officers who owned the private Trade Teas, have received for 6,454,947 pounds of Tea, which have been fold fince the 16th of September,	1,015,286
They would have received, if each fpecies of Tea had fold at that price at which the Eaft India Company faid they were willing to fell it,	863,564
Balance in favour of the Company and their Officers, - -	£. 151,723

It fhould be obferved, that I have not made any allowance for that fmall excefs of price, which was to be expected at the commencement of the new plan.

The fair Dealers in Tea have alfo their confolation: for the general increafe of bufinefs, in confequence of the alteration of duty, has been very confiderable. It is the Public, then, who have hitherto fuffered from a failure in the reduction of price: and it is the Public who ought to be principally confidered, in any mode which is pointed out for the correction of this failure.

The prefent failure of the Bill is to be corrected, by lowering the prices of Tea, till they correfpond with thofe that were held out to the Public. And this is, in my opinion, to be completely effected

by

by one, and only by one, method; which is, by the Company's having an ample quantity of Tea in this kingdom: let them but have this, and the Smuggler muft inevitably give way. It is in the power of *quantity* to reduce *price:* and I would never have the Company think that they have offered enough to fale, till the price is fufficiently reduced. Nor ought they (it will, I hope, be remembered, without my perpetually repeating it, that I am only delivering my *opinion.*) ever to reduce themfelves to the neceffity of putting up the whole quantity which they may have in their own warehoufes, of any fpecies of Tea. They ought always to have a Corps de réferve, to bring forward as occafion may require: and if either the Smuggler or the Speculator fhould appear—for they are both of them common enemies—I would have it advance.

The Eaft India Directors have it in their power to lower the prices, at which each fpecies of Tea is to be offered to fale. Of this power a good ufe may frequently be made: but it never can fuperfede the neceffity of an ample fupply. Such a quantity of any fpecies of Tea, as is inadequate to the demand for that fpecies, though it were put up (according to the Cuftom-houfe phrafe) at *nil,* would ftill fell for too much.

With refpect to any deviation from thofe prices which have been fixed at the public fale, and the Company's fubftituting, upon any condition whatever, more moderate prices, I confefs this is a plan which I cannot recommend. At prefent, the Com-

pany

pany have no power of felling, but by public fale: and to relinquifh the price which has been thus given, and to fix another, by private contract, would, I apprehend, be illegal.

It is true that the Company did, at the beginning of the firft part of the September Sale, permit the Buyers to relinquifh their purchafes : but the goods were again expofed to public fale.—Even this meafure, juftifiable, or, rather, commendable, as it was, upon fo fingular an occafion, ought not to be lightly repeated. For the confequence would be, that artful or indifcreet bidders would give high prices in hopes of a future reduction. Inftead of fuch an indulgence, they require to be taught, by that beft teacher Experience, a leffon of honefty and difcretion.

If the Company were to be allowed to fell their goods by private contract, or if the price at which they might fell them, were to be limited, even this would anfwer no end, unlefs they had an ample fupply : for if the Company fold an infufficient quantity at a low price, that infufficient quantity, the moment it had changed its owner, would, according to the natural courfe of trade, advance in value. The confumers would be nothing benefited. It will, perhaps, be faid, That if, as a Tea-dealer, I avowedly had bought my Tea cheap of the Company, I undoubtedly ought to fell it cheap; and not to comply with the advance of the market. This is plaufible theory : but the commercial practice has ever been to attend to the market price:

G   and

and as the holder of any article is obliged to sell that article for less than it cost him, if the market price of it be less, so, if the market price be more, he ought to be allowed to sell it for more. It is surely fair that this common principle of equity should be established between buyer and seller. But I will suppose, for a moment, that I had bought at any one Sale, or by private contract, as much Tea as would, according to my usual consumption, last me till the next Sale, or till any given period; and that, as soon as the Sale was over, or my purchase was made, the price of Tea suddenly and unexpectedly advanced in the market, and was raised by the dealer, in proportion to that advance: the East India Company declining to deliver, or being unable to deliver, any more Tea at so low a price as that which I had given. If I chose to stand single, or to be one of a few, and not to raise the price of my Teas, I might expect indeed a rapid demand for them; but that demand would presently exhaust my Stock, and oblige me to have recourse to the market.—Here would be an end of my patriotic supply, and I should begin to sell as my neighbours did, at a market price. Nothing then can *effectually* prevent this advance, and insure a continuance of low prices, but an *ample supply*. That will, I firmly believe, correct those high prices, and that present failure of the plan, which, for one, I seriously deplore.

Government has, indeed, been aware of the importance of this circumstance, and the Tea Act expressly exprefsly directs, as I have already obferved, that the Eaft India Company fhould have a Stock of Tea beforehand, equal to one year's confumption. They are, however, at prefent, far from having fuch a fupply, efpecially of Congou and Souchong Teas; and in thofe fpecies there has been the greateft excefs of price.

By noticing this fcarcity of Congou and Sou- chong Teas in the Company's warehoufes, I do not mean to cenfure the Directors for it. But I think it is abfolutely their duty—and I hope they will not be offended at the freedom with which I deliver my opinion upon this fubject—to provide themfelves with an ample fupply of each fpecies of Tea as foon as poffible. Fourteen Ships will probably arrive from China in the year 1786. The Seventeen Ships which are expected before that period will not, I am afraid, furnifh the Company with that abundance of each fpecies of Tea which they ought to have. The cafe, however, is not without hope of remedy. There are already large quantities of Tea upon the Continent: more are expected to arrive there; and from thofe quantities the Eaft India Company ought, if poffible, to fupply themfelves. This is a point which I have prefumed to urge upon every occafion: for I think it is a point of the moft unqueftionable policy, and of the utmoft importance. By purchafing the foreign Teas, the legal market will be furnifhed with that fupply which it fo much ftands in need of; and the illegal market will be deprived of its

grand

grand and cuſtomary ſource. Beſides this, we have been told, by indiſputable authority, that a very conſiderable quantity of the foreign Teas, has been offered to ſale much under prime coſt. By purchaſing this Tea, and by actually fixing a heavy loſs upon the original importers of it, the moſt effectual method would be taken of inducing them to give up their China Trade. But if, by ſuffering the moment of cheap purchaſe to eſcape, an opportunity ſhould be given to the owners of thoſe Teas of ſelling them much more advantageouſly, they might be thereby encouraged to renew their traffic. There is, indeed, reaſon to believe that the Eaſt India Directors have already purchaſed ſome of the Foreign Teas, (I fear at much higher prices than thoſe at which they might, at one time, have purchaſed them;) and I truſt they will nor neglect any opportunity of purchaſing more. Or if they ſhould be furniſhed with a ſufficient reaſon for not purchaſing them, they will, doubtleſs, in their juſtification, produce that reaſon to the Public. And if the Company ſhould ſtand in need of any pecuniary aſſiſtance, I ſhould think that the Public, who have not been backward upon ſuch occaſions, would readily aſſiſt them now, when it is ſo peculiarly their intereſt to do ſo. I would juſt add, that it ſeems to be particularly neceſſary for Government to exert themſelves, at this time, in the prevention of Smuggling, and to watch the Coaſt and the Counties upon it, as narrowly as poſſible. For the more difficulty and

danger

danger attend the practice of Smuggling, the more readily will the owners of foreign Teas difpofe of them upon moderate terms for the legal confumption of this Country.

I fhall now mention an alteration in the mode of putting up Teas to fale, which would, in my opinion, tend to reduce the price of them.

It has hitherto been cuftomary to divide the different fpecies of Tea, into lots containing different quantities. Singlo Tea, for example, is fold in lots containing either fix chefts or three chefts: Bohea in lots containing three chefts, two chefts, or one cheft: and it almoft conftantly happens, that the fmalleft lots fell at the higheft price. This is eafily to be accounted for. The fmall lots, by fuiting more perfons, admit more competitors than the large ones; and therefore they are ufually run up to a higher price. Every Sale Book, and, particularly, the book of the laft fale, will fufficiently confirm this fact.

As it appears, then, that the quantity contained in each lot has an effect upon its price, I would propofe that the quantity fhould be doubled. The prefent lots are proportioned to the annual fale of 6,000,000: and lots of double the fize will bear the fame proportion to the annual fale of 12,000,000. By thus encreafing the number of packages, which each lot is to contain, the Smuggler, who may be difpofed to bid upon, or even to buy, the three or four firft lots of any parcel of Tea, in order to keep up the price of it, will run a double rifk.

And

And thofe contefts, which too frequently take place in the Sale-room, even between fair buyers, or, as it more frequently happens, between the brokers whom they employ, would become more expenfive, and, confequently, more rare. Nor let the Public imagine that they have nothing to do with thefe contefts : for they often raife the price of the whole parcel, or, it may be, of the whole fpecies of Tea, about any lot or lots of which the difpute happens.

Having thus mentioned the principal reafons which induce me to recommend this alteration, I think it fair to acknowledge, that I have met with fome refpectable Dealers, who do not approve it. The only reafons which I recollect their having produced, in favour of their opinion, are, that it would give an unfair advantage to the large Dealer; and that as every advance of 1 d. per pound, would amount to more money upon a lot confifting of twelve Chefts, than it does upon a lot confifting of fix Chefts, the lofs would, if the purchafe were too dear, become greater.

As to the laft of thefe reafons, it is, as the reader muft have obferved, one of thofe which have induced me to propofe the alteration. If fome additional rifk fhould attend every advance, this evil may, by the exercife of additional caution, be converted into good : and I am perfuaded it would contribute to a reduction of price.

As to the other objection, viz. that of its giving an unfair advantage to the large Dealer, I can only fay, that if I thought it were likely to have this
tendency,

tendency, I would not recommend it: for I would have every person who was able to purchase one of the smallest lots under the old regulation, be able to purchase one of the smallest under the new: but I have already shewn, that the smallest lot, when doubled, would bear the same proportion to the whole consumption of legal Tea, which a lot of half the size did formerly. If, however, any fear or suspicion of injury to the small dealer should still remain, it might perhaps be entirely removed, by doubling the larger lots only, and leaving the smaller ones, as small as they now are. I really think this is not necessary: but still I would much rather it should be done unnecessarily, than that any act which has even the appearance of injustice or oppression, should take place.

The alteration which I propose would also tend to shorten the Sales: which—I speak feelingly—is a very desirable object to Tea-dealers: and, indeed, to the Public. We are to have at least five Sales in a year, (including the private Trade Sale): and I am sure that any person who is acquainted with the fatigue of Tea Sales, will not blame the Tea-dealers for wishing to curtail them. It is also of consequence to the Public: for when a Sale is once begun, it is certainly their interest to have the Teas sold, and delivered for their use, as soon as possible.

There is an allowance, in favour of the Public, which I apprehend the East India Directors can make, and which, in my opinion, it is reasonable they should make. I mean the customary allow-

ance

ance of Difcount, which ufed to be Six and an half
per cent.

This is a fubject, concerning which an un-
fuccefsful application was made to the Directors,
by the Tea-dealers, before the Tea Bill had
paffed. And left it fhould be thought that I now
renew the fubject, in the fpirit of vexation and dif-
appointment, I will briefly mention the reafon of
my doing fo. If it fhall appear to be a matter
which concerns the Public, I fhall be juftified.
If it fhould be thought that the Public have no
intereft in it, but that an allowance of Difcount
would prove beneficial to the Tea-dealer alone;
I fhall have to apologize for having given the Public any trouble upon the fubject.

An allowance of Six and an half per centum
upon the Sale Price of Teas had always been allowed by the Eaft India Company, to thofe purchafers, who fhould pay for their Goods upon the
firft prompt day, or day of payment.

In all the converfations which were held at the
Eaft India Houfe, relative to an alteration in the
price of Teas, it was conftantly underftood—I am
fure by myfelf, and I think I may fay by every
perfon in the Trade—that the cuftomary deduction
of Difcount would take place. Not a word was
faid upon the abolition of this allowance; and
therefore we might fairly infer its continuance.
When a copy of the Tea Bill was, by order of the
Houfe of Commons, printed, we were furprifed
to find, that we were likely to be deprived of our

4   Difcount,

Difcount. We had never heard of fuch a thing, we had never fufpected fuch a thing; and, to confefs the truth, we thought we had not been openly and handfomely treated in this matter. At a general meeting of the Dealers in Tea, it was unanimoufly refolved, that we fhould petition the Gentlemen in the Direction for our old allowance. Our Petition however was refufed; and the reafons which were given for the refufal were, " That in the prefent ftage of the Bill it would be highly inconvenient to make any alteration in the Prices; and alfo that the Court has it under confideration to abolifh the allowance of Difcount in general, therefore cannot comply with the requeft of the Tea-dealers to fell Tea hereafter fubject to Difcount."

We certainly did not think thefe were fufficient reafons for withdrawing the Difcount: and if they had been, in themfelves, fufficient, the circumftance ought furely to have been mentioned to us fooner. It was, however, ufelefs to remonftrate; and we were filent. I, for one, would have remained fo, if Teas had actually fold fo reafonably, that the confumer might purchafe them at the prices which he had been taught to expect. But fince there has undoubtedly been a great excefs of price, and fince the Eaft India Company have received from the Public a Sum, which fo far exceeded their expectation, it is furely equitable that they fhould give to the Public the cuftomary allowance of fix and an half per cent. There is not even the fhadow of a reafon for abolifhing

H

lifhing it, at the prefent high price. With refpect to the Sales that are over, this allowance cannot be made: the Company, and the owners of the private trade Teas, muft keep the fum of almoft 66,000 *l.* to which the Difcount upon thofe Sales would have amounted. I know not whether, under the prefent Act, the Eaft India Company can allow this Difcount upon the December Sale. If they can do it, I think they ought to do it: If they cannot, I think they ought to apply to Parliament, as foon as poffible, for fuch an alteration in the Act, as will enable them to allow Difcount hereafter.

Some perfons may imagine, that this allowance would make no difference to the Public, but would merely be added to the profit of the Tea-dealer. I believe it would happen, in fome inftances, that the Tea-dealers would fhare, and very fairly fhare, this allowance with the Public; but in general, the Public would reap the whole advantage: and in almoft all cafes the moft confiderable fhare of it. The profit which contents me now, would content me as well, if I had my old allowance of Difcount. I fhould certainly find that the Tea coft me fix and an half per cent. lefs for that allowance, and I fhould as certainly fell it to the Public fix and an half per cent. cheaper. Every Tea-dealer who means to content himfelf with a reafonable profit, and to fell Teas upon as advantageous terms as his neighbours, would doubtlefs do the fame.

I am

I am extremely defirous of proceeding one ftep further, and of endeavouring to provide for the Public fome confolation, though every effort which Government, the Eaft India Company, or the Tea-dealers can make, to reduce the Prices of Tea, fhould fail of producing the defired effect. It is no mean proof of good Generalfhip to draw advantage, even from the failure of a plan: and that is no defpicable Alchemy which converts a public lofs into Gold, for the ufe of the public treafury.

It is certain that great benefit was expected to refult to the Eaft India Company from the Tea Bill, even if the propofed reduction of price had immediately and completely taken place. Now the benefit which would have refulted from the *fuccefs* of the plan was all that the Company required: they declare it is all they wifh to have. Is it not then perfectly fair, that the *extra* fuccefs, which they reap at the expence of the Public, fhould be converted to the public emolument? Can the Eaft India Company, confiftently with their own declaration, refufe fuch an equitable appropriation of the public Money? This appears to me to be a plan of eafy and infallible accomplifhment. Certain average prices of each fpecies of Tea are held out to the Public, at which the Eaft India Company can avowedly afford to fell their Teas, and at which the Public have a right to expect that they fhould be fold. When the Eaft India Company have fixed upon the quantities of each fpecies of Tea which they mean to put up at any Sale, they have only to fee what fum of

money

money thofe quantities of Tea ought to bring into the Company's Treafury, reckoning each fpecies at that price for which the Company themfelves fay they *wifh* it to fell ; and at which the Public fay, they *expect* it to fell. Now whatever fum the Sale may produce, beyond that, which, according to the above fair mode of Calculation, it ought to do, is abfolutely fo much money paid, reluctantly, out of the pocket of the Public, and ought to be received, reluctantly, into the Treafury of the Company. To gratify each party, I would therefore propofe, that a Bill fhould be brought into Parliament to direct, that a very confiderable part of that fum, which I may call the Excefs of a Sale, fhould be applied, not to enrich the Eaft India Company, who have no equitable claim to it, but to the public fervice of the Kingdom. If my principle be good, it would, perhaps, warrant an application of the whole excefs to the purpofes of Government. But fo ftrict a rule as this, though it might be defended upon the ground of Equity, would not, I think, be perfectly confiftent with that fpirit of Liberality, which the Eaft India Company have fo often experienced from the Public.

As to that precife fhare of the excefs which ought to be refunded by the Eaft India Company to the Public, I fhall certainly leave that to be fuggefted by thofe, who are better qualified to fuggeft it. Nor fhall I prefume to fay, in what manner this fum ought to be applied by Government. I will only obferve, that as it fhould be looked upon as a Sum which is raifed from the Public,

4   and

and not as the bounty of the Eaft India Company, it ought to be applied in that way which will be moft vifibly to the public advantage.

It is not my intention to propofe an ex-poft-facto law, which fhall oblige the Eaft India Company to refund the very large fum which they received, beyond their expectation, from the Teas of laft Sale. I believe they neither expected, nor could prevent, the high prices which were then given: and if they take the earlieft opportunity of guarding the Public againft a fimilar lofs hereafter, they will probably be thought, by the Public, to have done all that it is now in their power to do. Nor is it merely at fuch a time as this, when the prices of Tea are avowedly much too high, that fuch a fecurity ought to be given to the Public. Circumftances may unexpectedly arife, even when the plan for reducing the prices of Tea, has been brought to perfection, which may caufe fuch an advance as would be detrimental to the Public. The Eaft India Company aim at a monopoly of Tea: and care fhould therefore be taken, that when they become Monopolifts, and there fhall be no European market, to which, in times of fcarcity, we can apply, they may not employ their power to the public difadvantage.

The act has taken care—and, indeed, very properly—that the Eaft India Company cannot be injured: they have a right to put up their Teas, at fuch prices, that they cannot lofe by them. Let the Public alfo be taken care of; and let any excefs of price, which they may at any time chance

to

to pay for their Teas, be converted, as it undoubtedly ought to be, to their own ufe.

As to the other objections which are made againſt the Tea Act, or rather, as I ought in this place to term it, againſt the Window Act, it is clear that the reduction of price would, in ſome degree, remove them: the pecuniary compenſation for the additional Window Tax would become greater; and the Public would, I hope, in conſideration of the other advantages of this Act, which I have endeavoured to enumerate, be reconciled to a Commutation, which, in a pecuniary view, ſhould not be completely adequate.

It appears to me to be perfectly equitable, though not, perhaps, perfectly popular, to diſtinguiſh the preſent enemies of the Tea Bill into two Claſſes. The one ſhould contain thoſe who had been accuſtomed to drink ſmuggled Tea: the other, the Conſumers of duty-paid Tea. It is certain that moſt of thoſe perſons who uſed to drink ſmuggled Tea will find themſelves much worſe off than they were before: but every complaint from that quarter, proves, not the injuſtice, but the equity and the Efficacy of the Bill: and the melancholy Fact, that at leaſt half the Tea which was conſumed in this Kingdom did not pay any duty at all, juſtifies our ſuppoſing that this Claſs of complainants muſt be very numerous.

I am, however, far from imagining, that every perſon who has been accuſtomed to ſupply himſelf with ſmuggled Tea, is become an enemy to the preſent Bill. There are doubtleſs many, who, notwithſtanding

withstanding they had recourse to an illegal market, whilst such a market notoriously existed, would cheerfully contribute a larger sum than that which the Tea Act will require from them, if, by so doing, they could crush a trade, which, they are ready to own, is most injurious to this Country. These persons will be satisfied, provided an equal market be established for all the consumers of Tea: but if there be two markets, they will have recourse to the cheapest.

The complaints which may come from the other class, undoubtedly merit the most serious attention; and ever will do so, till all just cause for those complaints shall be removed, by the actual accomplishment of that reduction of the price of Tea, which the Act gave us reason to expect.

If when the price of Tea shall be reduced as low as it ought to be, it should appear that the additional Window Tax is not raised as equitably as possible, but that it presses more hardly upon any particular class, than, in justice, it ought to do, I confess that this is an objection which deserves to be attended to, and to be removed: and if experience should point out a more equitable distribution of the Window Tax, or even a more eligible substitution for the duty which is taken off from Tea, I trust that the present Minister, or indeed any other, would be happy to adopt it.

I have not yet mentioned what would certainly remove, in an instant, most of the objections which are urged against the Tea Act: I mean its repeal, and the restoration of the old Tea duty: but

but this is a remedy, at which, divefting myfelf, as I think I can do, of my perfonal intereft as a Tea-dealer, I confefs I tremble. Of all the victo-ries which Smugglers have ever gained—and they have been too often victorious—this would be the moft fignal : the Revenue would probably receive fuch a wound that the expence of healing it might far exceed even the additional Window Tax : all the Eaft India Companies in Europe would flourifh —except our own : and bonfires would not only illumine the Britifh coaft, but alfo blaze on the Con-tinent, from the banks of the Tagus to the fhores of the Baltic. Befides, thofe perfons who anxioufly call out for a Repeal of the Tea Act, and who, to make ufe of their own expreffion, " wifh that things might be as they were before," feem to forget, that a repeal of the Tea Act would by no means place things in their former fituation. I believe I might venture to affert, that neither the old Window Tax, nor the old Duty upon Tea, would, now, bring in, any thing like what they formerly did. The Win-dow Tax certainly would not ; for the number of windows has, in confequence of the additional Tax, been very much reduced. A repeal of that ad-ditional Tax would not open all of them. And, with refpect to the Duty upon Tea, if, before perfons had been accuftomed to buy legal Tea at a low price, they were inclined to have recourfe to the Smuggler, they would be much more difpofed to do fo, when the great advance which would take place upon the prefent price of Teas, would point

out

out to them, more forcibly than ever, the advantage of Smuggling.

Having now pointed out, as well as I am able, those methods which are, in my opinion, moft likely to *correct* the *prefent failure* of the Tea Act; to *remove* the *principal objections* that are made to it; and to render it productive of the *good purpofes* for which it was framed, I have executed the tafk which I had undertaken.

With refpect to the manner in which it is executed, I am perfectly aware how much I fhall ftand in need of the public indulgence. Want of leifure is, it muft be confeffed, in general, a very trivial excufe: and he who prefumes to write for the *entertainment* of the Public, and has not leifure to write carefully, may juftly be afked, why he attempts to write at all. My object was, merely to convey to the Public, upon a fubject which fo much concerns them, all the information that it was in my power to give. And I truft their candour will make fome allowance for a perfon, who has literally been able to find no time for writing, except thofe hours, which, after the fatigue of Bufinefs, he has ftolen from reft. To the horæ fubfecivæ of the day, I have long been a ftranger.

In the courfe of my progrefs, I have had frequent occafion to confider the conduct of others. I have endeavoured to do this with a ftrict regard to truth: and I fhall be forry if, by the manner in which I have done it, I have rendered truth offenfive. I wifh to be treated with the fame

I   freedom,

freedom, with which I have treated others, I fhall acknowledge, without hefitation, the error of any opinion which I have delivered, as foon as I am convinced of it : and I fhall very gladly fee any information which I have given, difplaced by better. For as the facetious Knight valued himfelf, not only for his own wit, but alfo for that which he caufed in others, fo fhall I receive fatisfaction, not only from any ufeful information that I myfelf may have been able to give, but alfo from that better information which even my own errors may draw from others.

F I N I S.